Marketing
in the Digital Age

I0446465

By Rakesh Singh

Index

Chapter 1: Digital Marketing Fundamentals

Introduction

Welcome to the Digital Frontier

Begin the chapter with an engaging introduction, capturing the reader's attention by emphasizing the transformative nature of digital marketing in the business world. Convey the idea that understanding digital marketing fundamentals is crucial for anyone navigating this dynamic landscape.

Evolution of Marketing

Briefly trace the historical evolution of marketing from traditional methods to the digital era. Highlight key milestones, such as the advent of the internet, social media, and mobile technology, which have shaped the current state of digital marketing.

Section 1: The Core Principles of Digital Marketing

1. **Defining Digital Marketing**

   - Clearly define the term "digital marketing," emphasizing its broad scope, which includes various online channels and strategies.

Illustrate how digital marketing differs from traditional approaches and highlight its advantages in terms of reach, targeting, and measurability.

2. **Understanding the Customer Journey**

   - Explore the customer journey in the digital realm. Break down the stages from awareness to conversion, emphasizing the importance of delivering relevant content at each step. Discuss how understanding the customer journey informs effective digital marketing strategies.

3. **The Role of Targeting and Segmentation**

   - Dive into the concepts of audience targeting and segmentation. Explain how identifying and understanding the target audience allows marketers to create personalized campaigns, enhancing relevance and increasing the likelihood of engagement.

Section 2: Key Components of Digital Marketing

4. **Websites as Digital Hubs**

   - Discuss the pivotal role of websites in digital marketing. Highlight the importance of a well-designed, user-friendly website as the central hub for all digital marketing efforts. Emphasize the role of websites in establishing credibility and converting visitors into customers.

5. **Content as a Cornerstone**

   - Delve into the significance of content marketing. Explain how creating valuable and relevant content serves multiple purposes, including attracting organic traffic, engaging audiences on social media, and establishing thought leadership within the industry.

6. **Social Media's Impact**

   - Explore the vast landscape of social media platforms. Provide insights into the unique characteristics of major platforms and discuss best practices for leveraging social media to build brand awareness, engage audiences, and foster community.

7. **The Search Engine Ecosystem**

   - Introduce readers to the world of search engines and their impact on digital marketing. Discuss the basics of SEO and its role in improving a website's visibility on search engine results pages. Emphasize the importance of optimizing content for search engines.

Section 3: Metrics and Analytics

8. Measuring Success: Key Metrics

- Introduce readers to essential key performance indicators (KPIs) used in digital marketing. Explain how metrics such as website traffic, conversion rates, and engagement levels provide insights into the effectiveness of marketing efforts.

9. Google Analytics: A Deep Dive

- Walk readers through the basics of Google Analytics. Cover topics such as setting up an account, tracking website performance, and interpreting data. Highlight the valuable insights that Google Analytics can provide for refining digital marketing strategies.

Section 4: The Digital Marketing Toolbox

10. Tools and Technologies

- Provide an overview of the diverse tools and technologies available for digital marketers. Discuss marketing automation platforms, social media management tools, analytics tools, and other technologies that streamline and enhance digital marketing efforts.

Conclusion

Summarizing the Fundamentals

- Summarize the key concepts covered in the chapter, emphasizing the foundational principles of digital marketing. Reinforce the idea that a strong grasp of these fundamentals sets the stage for the exploration of more advanced digital marketing strategies in the subsequent chapters.

Chapter 2: The Digital Landscape: Trends and Insights

Introduction

Navigating the Rapidly Evolving Digital Ecosystem

Open the chapter by painting a vivid picture of the ever-shifting digital terrain. Express the need for marketers to be like skilled navigators, constantly adapting to new landscapes and leveraging emerging trends for success.

Section 1: Current Trends in Digital Marketing

Rise of Video Content

Explore the multifaceted role of video content in the contemporary digital landscape. Discuss the surge in video consumption across platforms and devices. Highlight the effectiveness of video in storytelling and engaging audiences. Provide statistics on the exponential growth of video content and its impact on user behavior.

Influencer Marketing Dynamics

Examine the evolution of influencer marketing into a powerful tool for brands. Discuss how influencers can humanize a brand, enhance credibility, and reach niche audiences. Provide insights into successful influencer collaborations and their measurable impact on brand awareness and conversion rates.

The Emergence of Ephemeral Content

Delve into the trend of ephemeral content and its impact on user engagement. Discuss the psychology behind temporary content and its effectiveness in creating a sense of urgency. Provide practical tips for crafting engaging and shareable ephemeral content. Highlight successful campaigns that leveraged Stories on various platforms.

Section 2: Emerging Technologies and Innovations

The Power of AI and Machine Learning

Explore the transformative role of AI and machine learning in reshaping digital marketing strategies. Discuss applications such as predictive analytics, chatbots for customer service, and personalized recommendations. Provide case studies illustrating how AI-driven campaigns have improved customer experiences and increased conversion rates.

Voice Search Optimization

Delve into the rise of voice search and its implications for marketers. Discuss the growing prevalence of voice-activated devices and how they are changing search behavior. Provide actionable insights on optimizing content for voice search, including the use of conversational keywords and structured data. Highlight successful voice search optimization strategies.**Augmented Reality (AR) and Virtual Reality (VR)**

Explore the immersive world of AR and VR and its impact on digital marketing. Discuss how brands are using augmented reality for interactive and engaging campaigns. Showcase examples of successful virtual reality experiences that have elevated brand storytelling and customer engagement.

Section 3: Data Privacy and Ethical Considerations

Navigating the Privacy Landscape

Examine the evolving landscape of data privacy regulations and consumer attitudes. Discuss the importance of compliance with privacy laws and the ethical use of customer data. Provide practical guidance on securing user consent, transparent data practices, and strategies for building trust in an era of heightened privacy concerns.

Ethical Marketing in the Digital Age

Explore the critical role of ethics in digital marketing. Discuss the impact of ethical practices on brand reputation and customer loyalty. Provide examples of brands that have successfully prioritized ethical marketing, showcasing how transparency and integrity contribute to long-term success.

Conclusion

Adapting to Change: A Blueprint for Success

Summarize the key trends and insights explored in the chapter. Reinforce the idea that staying informed about the dynamic digital landscape is essential for crafting successful marketing strategies. Tease how the following chapters will build upon these insights, providing practical guidance for marketers to navigate and capitalize on emerging trends.

Chapter 3: Crafting a Digital Strategy

Introduction

The Art of Strategy

Open the chapter by emphasizing the pivotal role of a well-defined digital strategy in achieving marketing objectives. Introduce the idea that crafting a digital strategy involves a thoughtful approach, aligning business goals with digital channels and tactics.

Section 1: Setting Objectives and Goals

Defining Clear Objectives

Discuss the importance of setting clear, measurable objectives for a digital marketing strategy. Explore common objectives, such as increasing brand awareness, driving website traffic, and boosting sales. Provide examples of SMART (Specific, Measurable, Achievable, Relevant, Time-bound) objectives for clarity.

Aligning with Business Goals

Emphasize the need for digital marketing objectives to align seamlessly with broader business goals. Discuss how a well-crafted digital strategy supports overall business growth, customer retention, and market expansion. Provide case studies illustrating successful alignment between digital strategies and business objectives.

Section 2: Understanding the Target Audience

Developing Buyer Personas

Guide readers through the process of creating detailed buyer personas. Explain how understanding the target audience's demographics, behaviors, and preferences informs content creation and channel selection. Provide templates and practical exercises for readers to develop their own buyer personas.

Analyzing Customer Journey Touchpoints

Explore the customer journey mapping process. Discuss the importance of identifying key touchpoints and understanding the customer's experience at each stage. Illustrate how mapping the customer journey enhances the precision of targeted digital marketing efforts.

Section 3: Selecting Digital Channels and Tactics

Leveraging Content Marketing

Delve into the role of content marketing within a digital strategy. Discuss the creation of high-quality, relevant content that resonates with the target audience. Explore different content formats, such as blog posts, videos, and infographics, and explain how to choose the most suitable formats for specific goals..

Social Media Integration

Discuss the strategic use of social media platforms. Explore how to choose the right platforms based on the target audience and business objectives. Provide insights into creating engaging social media content, building a community, and leveraging paid advertising on social channels.

Search Engine Optimization (SEO)

Examine the critical role of SEO in enhancing online visibility. Discuss on-page and off-page SEO strategies, keyword research, and the importance of a mobile-friendly website. Provide practical tips for optimizing content to improve search engine rankings.

Pay-Per-Click (PPC) Advertising

Explore the benefits of PPC advertising for driving targeted traffic. Discuss platforms like Google Ads and social media advertising. Provide a step-by-step guide to setting up effective PPC campaigns, including keyword selection, ad copywriting, and budget management.

Section 4: Measurement and Analytics

Establishing Key Performance Indicators (KPIs)

Discuss the importance of defining KPIs that align with digital marketing objectives. Explore common KPIs, such as website traffic, conversion rates, and social media engagement. Provide guidance on setting realistic benchmarks and goals for each KPI.

Utilizing Analytics Tools

Introduce readers to essential analytics tools for monitoring and evaluating digital marketing performance. Discuss the role of tools like Google Analytics, social media analytics, and SEO tools in tracking key metrics. Provide practical tips for interpreting data and making data-driven decisions.

Chapter 4: Content is King: Mastering Content Marketing

Introduction

The Power of Compelling Content

Begin the chapter by emphasizing the pivotal role of content in digital marketing. Introduce the concept that content is more than just information; it's a strategic asset that engages, informs, and drives audience action.

Section 1: Understanding Content Marketing

Defining Content Marketing

Explore the fundamentals of content marketing. Define content marketing as a strategic approach focused on creating and distributing valuable, relevant, and consistent content to attract and retain a clearly defined audience.

The Role of Storytelling

Discuss the importance of storytelling in content marketing. Explore how compelling narratives resonate with audiences on an emotional level, making brands more memorable.

Provide examples of successful storytelling in digital marketing campaigns.

Section 2: Creating High-Quality Content

Identifying Your Unique Voice

Guide readers in finding and defining their brand's unique voice. Discuss how a distinct voice contributes to brand identity and helps create a consistent and recognizable presence across all content.

Understanding Your Audience's Needs

Delve into audience-centric content creation. Explore techniques for understanding audience needs, preferences, and pain points. Discuss the importance of creating content that provides value, answers questions, and addresses the challenges of the target audience.

Diversifying Content Formats

Examine the various content formats available to marketers. Discuss the benefits of diversifying content, including blog posts, videos, infographics, podcasts, and more. Provide guidance on selecting the most effective formats for different goals and audience preferences.

Section 3: Content Distribution Strategies

Leveraging Social Media Channels

Explore the role of social media in content distribution. Discuss strategies for promoting content on platforms like Facebook, Instagram, Twitter, and LinkedIn. Provide tips for creating shareable content and fostering community engagement.

Email Marketing Excellence

Examine the use of email as a powerful content distribution channel. Discuss strategies for building and segmenting email lists, crafting compelling email content, and measuring email marketing performance.

Search Engine Optimization (SEO) for Content

Delve into the relationship between content and SEO. Explore the principles of optimizing content for search engines, including keyword research, on-page SEO techniques, and the importance of high-quality, relevant content for improved search rankings.

Section 4: Measuring Content Effectiveness

Defining Key Content Metrics

Introduce key performance indicators (KPIs) for measuring content effectiveness. Discuss metrics such as page views, time on page, social shares, and conversion rates. Explain how these metrics align with overall content marketing goals.

Utilizing Analytics Tools for Insights

Explore the use of analytics tools to gain insights into content performance. Discuss the role of tools like Google Analytics, social media analytics, and email marketing analytics in tracking and analyzing content metrics.

Section 5: Content Planning and Editorial Calendar

Developing a Content Calendar

Guide readers through the process of creating a content calendar. Discuss the benefits of planning content in advance, ensuring consistency, and aligning with overarching marketing goals. Provide a template or framework for readers to organize their content calendar effectively.

Aligning Content with the Buyer's Journey

Explore how content can be strategically aligned with the stages of the buyer's journey—awareness, consideration, and decision. Discuss the types of content that resonate at each stage and provide examples of successful content mapping.

Section 6: User-Generated Content and Community Building

Harnessing the Power of User-Generated Content (UGC)

Examine the role of user-generated content in content marketing. Discuss strategies for encouraging and curating user-generated content, including customer testimonials, reviews, and social media contributions. Highlight successful campaigns that leveraged UGC for brand promotion.

Building a Digital Community

Discuss the importance of building a community around content. Explore how engaging with the audience through comments, forums, and social media fosters a sense of belonging. Provide tips for community building and sustaining meaningful interactions.

Section 7: Interactive Content and Emerging Formats

Exploring Interactive Content

Delve into the realm of interactive content. Discuss the effectiveness of quizzes, polls, surveys, and interactive infographics in engaging audiences. Provide guidance on incorporating interactive elements to enhance user experience and capture valuable data.

Emerging Content Formats: VR and AR

Explore the potential of virtual reality (VR) and augmented reality (AR) in content marketing. Discuss how brands are using immersive experiences to tell stories and connect with audiences. Provide examples of successful VR and AR content marketing campaigns.

Section 8: Content Repurposing and Evergreen Strategies

Repurposing Content for Multiple Platforms

Examine the strategy of repurposing content across different platforms. Discuss how one piece of content can be adapted into various formats, such as blog posts, videos, and social media snippets. Provide a guide on repurposing content effectively.

Evergreen Content: Creating Timeless Assets

Explore the concept of evergreen content and its role in sustaining long-term visibility. Discuss how to create content that remains relevant over time and continues to attract organic traffic. Provide examples of evergreen content that consistently performs well.

Section 9: International and Multilingual Content

Global Reach: Content for International Audiences

Discuss the considerations for creating content for international audiences. Explore the importance of cultural sensitivity, language preferences, and regional nuances. Provide insights into global content strategies and successful examples of international content campaigns.

Conclusion

The Art and Science of Content Mastery

Summarize the key elements discussed in the chapter, emphasizing the multifaceted nature of content marketing. Reinforce the idea that mastering content marketing is both an art and a science that requires creativity, strategy, and ongoing adaptation. Conclude by highlighting the central role of content in building meaningful connections with audiences in the digital landscape.

Chapter 5: Social Media Mastery

Introduction

The Social Media Landscape

Open the chapter by highlighting the central role of social media in modern digital marketing. Introduce the idea that social media is a dynamic and influential platform for brand communication, community building, and audience engagement.

Section 1: Strategic Social Media Planning

Defining Social Media Objectives

Discuss the importance of defining clear objectives for social media efforts. Explore objectives such as brand awareness, community building, lead generation, and customer engagement. Provide examples of well-defined social media objectives.

Identifying Target Social Media Platforms

Guide readers through the process of selecting the most suitable social media platforms for their brand. Discuss the demographics, user behavior, and features of major platforms such as Facebook, Instagram, Twitter, LinkedIn, and TikTok.

Developing a Social Media Content Strategy

Explore the principles of crafting a comprehensive social media content strategy. Discuss the importance of varied content types, including text, images, videos, and infographics. Provide insights into maintaining a consistent brand voice across different platforms.

Section 2: Content Creation and Branding

Creating Engaging Visual Content

Delve into the creation of visually appealing content for social media. Discuss the impact of high-quality images, graphics, and videos in capturing audience attention. Provide tips for optimizing visuals for each platform's specifications.

Crafting Compelling Copy

Explore the art of writing effective social media copy. Discuss the importance of concise and engaging messaging. Provide examples of successful copywriting techniques for different social media contexts, such as captions, tweets, and LinkedIn posts.

Maintaining Brand Consistency

Discuss the significance of consistent branding across social media channels. Explore how cohesive visual elements, messaging, and tone contribute to brand recognition. Provide practical tips for maintaining brand consistency on each platform.

Section 3: Community Engagement and Influencer Collaboration

Building and Nurturing Communities

Discuss the importance of community engagement on social media. Explore strategies for fostering conversations, responding to comments, and creating a sense of community around a brand. Provide examples of successful community-building initiatives.

Leveraging Influencer Marketing

Explore the role of influencers in social media marketing. Discuss the benefits of collaborating with influencers, from expanding reach to building credibility. Provide guidance on identifying and partnering with influencers relevant to the brand.

Section 4: Social Media Advertising

Introduction to Social Media Advertising

Examine the role of paid advertising on social media platforms. Discuss the advantages of social media advertising, including precise targeting, analytics, and various ad formats. Provide an overview of major social media advertising platforms.

Creating Effective Social Media Ads

Guide readers through the process of creating compelling social media ads. Discuss elements such as visuals, ad copy, calls-to-action, and targeting options. Provide tips for optimizing ad performance and measuring ad success.

Section 5: Analytics and Performance Measurement

Key Social Media Metrics

Introduce readers to essential social media metrics for performance measurement. Discuss metrics such as reach, engagement, click-through rates, and conversion tracking. Emphasize the importance of aligning metrics with social media objectives.

Utilizing Social Media Analytics Tools

Explore the use of analytics tools for social media performance analysis. Discuss popular tools like Facebook Insights, Instagram Analytics, and Twitter Analytics. Provide practical insights into interpreting data and adjusting strategies based on analytics.

Section 6: Realistic Social Media Planning

Setting Achievable Social Media Goals

Encourage readers to set realistic and achievable social media goals. Emphasize the importance of aligning goals with the brand's current standing and resources. Provide examples of incremental goals that contribute to broader objectives over time.

Understanding Platform Nuances

Delve into the nuanced characteristics of each social media platform. Discuss how user behavior, content preferences, and engagement styles vary across platforms. Provide realistic expectations for growth and engagement based on the nature of each platform.

Adapting Content for Each Platform

Guide readers in tailoring content for specific social media platforms. Discuss the importance of adapting content formats and messaging to match the preferences of each audience. Provide examples of brands successfully customizing content for different platforms.

Section 7: Authentic Community Building

Fostering Genuine Conversations

Highlight the value of authentic conversations on social media. Discuss strategies for fostering genuine interactions, responding to comments, and addressing customer inquiries. Provide real-world examples of brands effectively engaging with their communities.

Nurturing User-Generated Content

Explore realistic approaches to encouraging user-generated content. Discuss strategies such as contests, challenges, and hashtag campaigns. Share examples of brands that have successfully leveraged user-generated content to strengthen their online presence.

Section 8: Micro-Influencers and Niche Collaboration

Embracing Micro-Influencer Partnerships

Discuss the realistic benefits of collaborating with micro-influencers. Highlight how these influencers often have more engaged and niche audiences, making them valuable for certain brands. Provide guidance on identifying and building relationships with micro-influencers.

Niche Marketing Strategies

Explore the concept of niche marketing on social media. Discuss the advantages of targeting specific niches and tailoring content to niche audiences. Provide examples of brands that have succeeded by embracing niche strategies in their social media marketing.

Section 9: Cost-Effective Social Media Advertising

Budget-Friendly Advertising Approaches

Discuss cost-effective social media advertising strategies for businesses with limited budgets. Explore options such as targeted boosting, carousel ads, and strategic ad placements. Provide practical tips for maximizing the impact of advertising investments.

DIY Ad Creation Tips

Guide readers through the process of creating DIY social media ads. Discuss tools and resources for designing eye-catching visuals and compelling copy. Provide insights into optimizing ad performance without the need for extensive design skills.

Section 10: Meaningful Social Media Analytics

Setting Realistic Expectations for Metrics

Help readers set realistic expectations for social media metrics. Discuss industry benchmarks and provide context for interpreting performance metrics based on the brand's size, industry, and target audience.

Practical Insights from Analytics

Explore how to derive actionable insights from social media analytics. Discuss not only the numbers but also the story they tell about audience behavior, content effectiveness, and overall social media strategy. Provide examples of adjustments made based on data-driven insights.

Conclusion

Social Media Mastery: Balancing Realism and Ambition

Summarize the chapter, highlighting the balance between realistic expectations and ambitious goals in social media mastery. Emphasize that success on social media is a journey that requires adaptability, authenticity, and a keen understanding of the platform dynamics. Conclude by encouraging readers to apply the principles discussed in the chapter to their unique brand context.

Chapter 6: Search Engine Optimization (SEO): Navigating the Digital Landscape

Introduction

The Crucial Role of SEO

Begin the chapter by emphasizing the critical role of SEO in digital marketing. Introduce the concept that SEO is the backbone of online visibility, driving organic traffic and ensuring a brand's discoverability in search engine results.

Section 1: Understanding the Foundations of SEO

Defining SEO and Its Evolution

Explore the definition and evolution of SEO. Discuss how SEO has transformed from keyword stuffing to a holistic approach that encompasses content quality, user experience, and technical optimization. Provide a historical overview of key algorithm updates.

The Importance of Keyword Research

Delve into the significance of keyword research in SEO. Discuss how identifying relevant keywords aligns with user intent and search queries. Provide practical insights into conducting keyword research using tools like Google Keyword Planner and SEMrush.

On-Page SEO Best Practices

Discuss on-page SEO elements that contribute to a website's visibility. Explore the optimization of title tags, meta descriptions, header tags, and URL structures. Provide a checklist for readers to implement on-page SEO best practices.

Section 2: Technical SEO Essentials

Website Structure and Navigation

Explore the role of website structure in SEO. Discuss how a well-organized site structure and intuitive navigation contribute to user experience and search engine crawlability. Provide tips for optimizing site architecture.

Mobile Optimization

Examine the importance of mobile optimization for SEO. Discuss the prevalence of mobile searches and how search engines prioritize mobile-friendly websites. Provide practical insights into creating responsive designs and optimizing for mobile users.

Page Speed and Performance

Delve into the impact of page speed on SEO and user experience. Discuss the importance of fast-loading pages for search engine rankings and user satisfaction. Provide tips for optimizing images, leveraging browser caching, and minimizing HTTP requests.

Section 3: Content Strategies for SEO

High-Quality Content Creation

Discuss the central role of high-quality content in SEO. Explore how search engines prioritize valuable, relevant, and well-crafted content. Provide guidance on creating content that satisfies user intent and fulfills search queries.

Content Optimization Techniques

Explore content optimization techniques for SEO. Discuss the strategic use of keywords, headers, and multimedia elements within content. Provide examples of well-optimized content that ranks prominently in search results.

Long-Form and Evergreen Content

Discuss the benefits of long-form and evergreen content for SEO. Explore how in-depth articles and timeless content contribute to higher search engine rankings and sustained organic traffic. Provide tips for creating comprehensive, evergreen content.

Section 4: Link Building and Off-Page SEO

The Significance of Backlinks

Examine the importance of backlinks in SEO. Discuss how quality backlinks from reputable sources signal authority and trust to search engines. Provide insights into ethical link-building strategies and the pitfalls of manipulative practices.

Social Signals and Brand Mentions

Explore the role of social signals and brand mentions in off-page SEO. Discuss how social media activity and online mentions contribute to a brand's online authority. Provide tips for fostering positive social signals.

Section 5: SEO Analytics and Measurement

Key SEO Metrics

Introduce readers to key SEO metrics for performance measurement. Discuss metrics such as organic traffic, keyword rankings, click-through rates, and conversion rates. Provide guidance on setting realistic benchmarks for SEO success.

Utilizing SEO Analytics Tools

Explore the use of SEO analytics tools for monitoring and analyzing performance. Discuss popular tools like Google Analytics, Google Search Console, and third-party SEO platforms. Provide practical tips for leveraging these tools to refine SEO strategies.

Section 6: Local SEO Strategies

The Importance of Local SEO

Discuss the significance of local SEO for businesses with a physical presence. Explore how local SEO enhances visibility in local search results, Google Maps, and location-based searches. Provide practical insights into optimizing for local search.

Google My Business Optimization

Guide readers through the process of optimizing their Google My Business (GMB) profiles. Discuss the impact of accurate business information, reviews, and photos on local search rankings. Provide tips for encouraging and managing customer reviews.

Section 7: SEO for E-Commerce

E-Commerce SEO Essentials

Examine the unique challenges and opportunities of SEO for e-commerce websites. Discuss strategies for optimizing product pages, handling duplicate content, and improving the overall user experience. Provide examples of successful e-commerce SEO implementations.

Product Page Optimization

Delve into the specifics of optimizing individual product pages for SEO. Discuss the importance of high-quality product descriptions, user reviews, and structured data. Provide guidance on creating compelling product page content that aligns with search intent.

Section 8: SEO in a Mobile-First World

Mobile-First Indexing

Explore the shift toward mobile-first indexing and its implications for SEO. Discuss how search engines prioritize mobile-friendly content and the impact on search rankings. Provide insights into optimizing content for mobile devices.

Voice Search Optimization

Examine the rising prominence of voice search and its impact on SEO. Discuss how voice search queries differ from text-based searches and provide practical tips for optimizing content for voice search. Explore the role of featured snippets in voice search results.

Section 9: SEO Trends and Future Considerations

Emerging SEO Trends

Discuss current and emerging trends in the field of SEO. Explore topics such as the rise of video SEO, the impact of artificial intelligence on search algorithms, and the evolving nature of user search behavior. Provide insights into staying ahead of SEO trends.

Future Considerations in SEO

Explore potential future developments in SEO. Discuss the evolving role of machine learning, the influence of user experience on search rankings, and the impact of emerging technologies. Encourage readers to stay informed and adapt their SEO strategies accordingly.

Conclusion

Navigating the Ever-Changing SEO Landscape

Summarize the key takeaways from the chapter, emphasizing that SEO is a dynamic field that requires continuous learning and adaptation. Reinforce the idea that mastering SEO involves a combination of technical expertise, content optimization, and staying attuned to industry trends. Conclude by highlighting the long-term value of effective SEO in navigating the ever-changing digital landscape.

Chapter 7: Pay-Per-Click (PPC) Advertising: Strategic Campaigns for Results

Introduction

The Power of PPC Advertising

Begin the chapter by highlighting the significance of Pay-Per-Click (PPC) advertising in the digital marketing landscape. Introduce the concept that PPC offers a targeted and measurable approach to drive immediate results and maximize return on investment (ROI).

Section 1: Understanding the Fundamentals of PPC

Defining PPC Advertising

Explore the fundamental principles of PPC advertising. Discuss how advertisers pay a fee each time their ad is clicked, making it a cost-effective way to drive traffic and conversions. Provide an overview of popular PPC platforms, such as Google Ads and Bing Ads.

Keyword Research for PPC

Delve into the importance of keyword research in PPC campaigns. Discuss how selecting relevant keywords aligns with user intent and influences ad visibility. Provide practical insights into conducting effective keyword research for PPC.

Ad Copywriting Strategies

Explore the art of crafting compelling ad copy for PPC campaigns. Discuss the importance of concise and persuasive messaging. Provide tips for creating attention-grabbing headlines, compelling ad descriptions, and effective calls-to-action.

Section 2: PPC Campaign Structure and Settings

Campaign Structure Overview

Guide readers through the structure of a well-organized PPC campaign. Discuss the hierarchy of campaigns, ad groups, and keywords. Provide insights into creating a logical and strategic campaign structure for optimal performance.

Budgeting and Bidding Strategies

Examine the considerations for budgeting and bidding in PPC advertising. Discuss how setting realistic budgets and strategic bidding contribute to campaign success. Provide tips for optimizing bidding strategies to achieve specific goals.

Ad Extensions and Enhancements

Discuss the role of ad extensions in enhancing PPC ads. Explore various ad extensions, such as site link extensions, callout extensions, and structured snippet extensions. Provide guidance on utilizing ad extensions to improve ad visibility and user engagement.

Section 3: Targeting and Audience Segmentation

Geographic and Demographic Targeting

Explore the importance of geographic and demographic targeting in PPC campaigns. Discuss how targeting specific locations and audience demographics improves relevance and increases the likelihood of conversion. Provide tips for optimizing geographic and demographic settings.

Audience Segmentation Strategies

Delve into audience segmentation strategies for PPC advertising. Discuss the use of audience data to create targeted campaigns for different customer segments. Provide insights into leveraging remarketing and custom audiences for enhanced targeting.

Section 4: Ad Performance Monitoring and Optimization

Key Performance Indicators (KPIs) in PPC

Introduce readers to essential Key Performance Indicators (KPIs) for measuring PPC success. Discuss metrics such as click-through rate (CTR), conversion rate, and cost per conversion. Provide guidance on setting realistic KPI benchmarks.

Utilizing PPC Analytics Tools

Explore the use of analytics tools for monitoring and optimizing PPC performance. Discuss platforms like Google Ads and Bing Ads analytics. Provide practical tips for interpreting data and making data-driven decisions to enhance campaign effectiveness.

Section 5: Advanced PPC Strategies

A/B Testing for Ad Performance

Discuss the importance of A/B testing in PPC advertising. Explore how testing different ad elements, such as headlines, images, and calls-to-action, provides valuable insights into audience preferences. Provide a guide to conducting effective A/B tests.

Dynamic and Shopping Campaigns

Delve into advanced PPC campaign types, such as dynamic search ads and shopping campaigns. Discuss how dynamic campaigns automatically target relevant search queries and how shopping campaigns showcase products directly in search results. Provide tips for implementing and optimizing these advanced campaign types.

Section 6: Budget Optimization and ROI

Strategic Budget Allocation

Guide readers through the process of optimizing their PPC budget for maximum ROI. Discuss the importance of allocating budget to high-performing keywords, ad groups, and campaigns. Provide insights into adjusting budgets based on performance trends.

Calculating and Improving ROI

Explore methods for calculating Return on Investment (ROI) in PPC campaigns. Discuss the factors that contribute to ROI, including ad spend, conversions, and customer lifetime value. Provide practical tips for improving ROI through strategic adjustments.

Section 7: Adapting to Seasonal Trends

Understanding Seasonal PPC Trends

Discuss the impact of seasonal trends on PPC advertising. Explore how consumer behavior shifts during peak seasons and holidays. Provide strategies for adapting PPC campaigns to capitalize on seasonal trends, including adjusting ad copy and targeting.

Holiday-Specific Campaigns

Delve into the planning and execution of holiday-specific PPC campaigns. Discuss the importance of creating festive ad creatives, leveraging promotions, and optimizing bidding strategies for holiday traffic. Provide examples of successful holiday PPC campaigns.

Section 8: Video Advertising and Social PPC

The Rise of Video Advertising

Explore the role of video advertising in PPC campaigns. Discuss the effectiveness of video ads in capturing audience attention and conveying brand messages. Provide insights into creating compelling video content for PPC

Social Media PPC Campaigns

Examine the integration of PPC advertising with social media platforms. Discuss the unique features and targeting options available on platforms like Facebook, Instagram, and LinkedIn. Provide tips for creating successful social PPC campaigns.

Section 9: Ethical Considerations and Compliance

Ad Copy Compliance

Discuss the importance of ensuring ad copy compliance with platform policies. Explore common issues related to ad content, claims, and prohibited practices. Provide guidance on creating ethical and compliant PPC ad copy.

Transparency in Data Usage

Explore the ethical use of data in PPC advertising. Discuss privacy concerns and the importance of transparent data practices. Provide insights into building trust with users by clearly communicating data usage policies.

Section 10: Future Trends in PPC

Emerging Technologies in PPC

Discuss current and emerging trends in PPC advertising. Explore topics such as the impact of machine learning on ad targeting, the rise of augmented reality (AR) ads, and the integration of voice search in PPC. Provide insights into staying ahead of PPC trends.

The Evolution of Paid Search

Examine potential future developments in paid search. Discuss how advancements in search engine algorithms, user behavior, and technology may shape the future of PPC. Encourage readers to stay informed and adapt their PPC strategies to evolving trends.

Conclusion

PPC Mastery: A Dynamic Journey

Summarize the key takeaways from the chapter, emphasizing that PPC mastery involves continuous adaptation to industry trends, strategic campaign planning, and ethical considerations. Reinforce the idea that PPC is a dynamic and evolving field that requires ongoing learning and optimization. Conclude by highlighting the enduring value of PPC in achieving measurable results for businesses in the digital era.

Chapter 8: Data-Driven Decision-Making: Transforming Insights into Action

Introduction

The Power of Data-Driven Decision-Making

Begin the chapter by emphasizing the transformative impact of data-driven decision-making in digital marketing. Introduce the concept that leveraging data insights allows businesses to make informed, strategic decisions that drive success in the dynamic online landscape.

Section 1: The Role of Data in Digital Marketing

Defining Data-Driven Decision-Making

Explore the definition and significance of data-driven decision-making. Discuss how it involves using data analysis to inform business strategies and marketing initiatives. Provide examples of successful companies that prioritize data-driven approaches.

Types of Data in Digital Marketing

Delve into the various types of data relevant to digital marketing. Discuss customer data, performance metrics, demographic data, and behavioral data. Provide insights into how each type of data contributes to a comprehensive understanding of the target audience and marketing effectiveness.

Section 2: Implementing a Data-Driven Culture

Building a Data-Driven Culture

Discuss the importance of fostering a data-driven culture within an organization. Explore how this involves encouraging employees at all levels to use data in decision-making. Provide tips for creating an environment where data is valued and utilized.

Overcoming Data-Driven Challenges

Examine common challenges organizations face in becoming truly data-driven. Discuss issues such as data silos, lack of skills, and resistance to change. Provide strategies for overcoming these challenges and promoting a seamless integration of data into decision-making processes.

Section 3: Collecting and Analyzing Data

Data Collection Strategies

Guide readers through effective data collection strategies in digital marketing. Discuss the use of analytics tools, customer surveys, and feedback mechanisms. Provide insights into selecting the most relevant data sources based on business goals.

Data Analysis Techniques

Delve into data analysis techniques that transform raw data into actionable insights. Discuss approaches such as descriptive analytics, diagnostic analytics, predictive analytics, and prescriptive analytics. Provide examples of how each technique contributes to decision-making.

Section 4: Personalization and Targeting with Data

Personalization Strategies

Explore how data-driven insights enable personalized marketing strategies. Discuss the importance of tailoring content, offers, and experiences based on individual customer preferences. Provide examples of successful personalization in digital marketing campaigns.

Targeted Advertising and Segmentation

Discuss the role of data in targeted advertising and audience segmentation. Explore how demographic, behavioral, and contextual data can inform precise targeting. Provide insights into creating effective segmentation strategies for different marketing channels.

Section 5: Optimization and Continuous Improvement

A/B Testing and Experimentation

Examine the role of A/B testing and experimentation in data-driven optimization. Discuss how testing different variables, such as headlines, visuals, and calls-to-action, helps identify the most effective strategies. Provide a guide to implementing successful A/B testing.

Performance Monitoring and KPIs

Explore the ongoing process of performance monitoring using key performance indicators (KPIs). Discuss the importance of aligning KPIs with business objectives and adjusting strategies based on performance metrics. Provide practical tips for establishing and tracking KPIs.

Conclusion

Data-Driven Decision-Making: A Strategic Imperative

Summarize the key concepts discussed in the chapter, emphasizing that data-driven decision-making is a strategic imperative for success in digital marketing. Reinforce the idea that leveraging data empowers organizations to stay agile, optimize campaigns, and meet evolving customer expectations. Conclude by highlighting the enduring value of a data-driven approach in navigating the complexities of the digital landscape.

Chapter 9: Email Marketing: Crafting Effective Campaigns for Engagement and Conversions

Introduction

The Enduring Power of Email Marketing

Begin the chapter by highlighting the enduring effectiveness of email marketing in the digital landscape. Introduce the concept that, when done strategically, email marketing remains a powerful tool for building relationships, nurturing leads, and driving conversions.

Section 1: Email Marketing Fundamentals

Defining Email Marketing

Explore the fundamental principles of email marketing. Discuss how it involves sending targeted messages to a group of individuals with the goal of building relationships, promoting products or services, and driving specific actions. Provide examples of successful email marketing campaigns.

Building an Email List

Delve into the importance of building and maintaining a quality email list. Discuss strategies for growing an email subscriber base, including lead magnets, opt-in forms, and incentives. Provide insights into the value of a segmented and engaged email list.

Section 2: Creating Compelling Email Content

Crafting Engaging Email Copy

Explore the art of writing compelling email copy. Discuss the importance of creating attention-grabbing subject lines, personalized greetings, and persuasive content. Provide examples of effective email copywriting techniques.

Visual Elements in Email Design

Delve into the role of visual elements in email design. Discuss the impact of eye-catching graphics, images, and layouts in enhancing the visual appeal of emails. Provide practical tips for optimizing email design for various devices

Section 3: Email Campaign Strategy

Types of Email Campaigns

Discuss various types of email campaigns and their purposes. Explore promotional campaigns, newsletters, welcome series, abandoned cart emails, and more. Provide insights into when to deploy each type of campaign for maximum impact.

Automating Email Sequences

Examine the benefits of automating email sequences. Discuss how automation streamlines communication, nurtures leads, and drives conversions. Provide examples of effective automated email sequences, including drip campaigns and triggered messages.

Section 4: Personalization and Segmentation

Personalizing Email Campaigns

Explore the role of personalization in email marketing. Discuss how tailoring content based on subscriber preferences, behaviors, and demographics enhances engagement. Provide insights into dynamic content, personalized recommendations, and user-specific messaging.

Segmentation Strategies

Delve into the importance of segmentation in email marketing. Discuss how segmenting an email list based on criteria such as location, purchase history, and engagement level allows for targeted and relevant communication. Provide guidance on effective segmentation strategies.

Section 5: Metrics and Analytics in Email Marketing

Key Email Marketing Metrics

Introduce readers to key metrics for measuring the success of email marketing campaigns. Discuss metrics such as open rates, click-through rates, conversion rates, and unsubscribe rates. Provide insights into how each metric contributes to campaign evaluation.

Utilizing Email Analytics Tools

Explore the use of email analytics tools for monitoring and optimizing campaign performance. Discuss popular email marketing platforms and third-party analytics tools. Provide practical tips for interpreting data and refining email strategies based on analytics.

Section 6: Advanced Email Marketing Strategies

Interactive and Dynamic Content

Examine advanced strategies for incorporating interactive and dynamic content in emails. Discuss how features like surveys, polls, and real-time content updates enhance user engagement. Provide examples of brands successfully using interactive elements in their email campaigns.

User-generated Content (UGC) in Emails

Explore the inclusion of user-generated content in email campaigns. Discuss the impact of featuring customer reviews, testimonials, and user-submitted content. Provide insights into leveraging UGC to build trust and authenticity.

Section 7: Email Deliverability and Compliance

Ensuring High Email Deliverability

Discuss the importance of email deliverability in email marketing success. Explore strategies for maintaining high deliverability rates, including list hygiene, authentication, and compliance with email regulations. Provide tips for avoiding common pitfalls that can affect deliverability.

Compliance with Email Regulations

Examine the legal and ethical considerations in email marketing. Discuss compliance with regulations such as CAN-SPAM Act and GDPR. Provide guidance on obtaining consent, honoring unsubscribe requests, and ensuring transparency in email communications.

Section 8: Email Marketing Trends

Emerging Trends in Email Marketing

Discuss current and emerging trends in email marketing. Explore topics such as the rise of artificial intelligence in email personalization, interactive email experiences, and the integration of email with other marketing channels. Provide insights into staying ahead of email marketing trends.

Mobile Optimization for Emails

Examine the importance of mobile optimization in email marketing. Discuss the prevalence of mobile email opens and the impact of responsive design on user experience. Provide tips for optimizing emails for mobile devices to enhance readability and engagement.

Section 9: Email Marketing Challenges and Solutions

Overcoming Common Challenges

Examine common challenges faced by email marketers. Discuss issues such as low open rates, high unsubscribe rates, and maintaining engagement over time. Provide practical solutions and strategies for overcoming these challenges.

Customer Retention through Email

Explore the role of email marketing in customer retention. Discuss strategies for nurturing ongoing relationships with existing customers through targeted email campaigns. Provide examples of successful customer retention email programs.

Conclusion

The Ever-Evolving Landscape of Email Marketing

Summarize the key takeaways from the chapter, emphasizing that email marketing is a dynamic and ever-evolving discipline. Reinforce the idea that mastery in email marketing involves a combination of creative content, strategic planning, compliance, and adaptation to emerging trends. Conclude by highlighting the enduring value of email marketing in building meaningful connections with an audience.

Chapter 10: Integrated Marketing Strategies: Harmonizing Channels for Maximum Impact

Introduction

The Power of Integration in Marketing

Begin the chapter by highlighting the significance of integrated marketing strategies. Introduce the concept that an integrated approach, harmonizing various marketing channels, maximizes impact and creates a cohesive brand experience for the audience.

Section 1: Understanding Integrated Marketing

Defining Integrated Marketing

Explore the definition of integrated marketing. Discuss how it involves aligning and coordinating various marketing channels to deliver a unified message and brand experience. Provide examples of successful integrated marketing campaigns.

Benefits of Integration

Delve into the benefits of adopting an integrated marketing approach. Discuss how integration enhances brand consistency, improves audience engagement, and maximizes the overall effectiveness of marketing efforts. Provide insights into achieving synergy across channels.

Section 2: Cross-Channel Coordination

Identifying Key Marketing Channels

Discuss the various marketing channels available, including digital, social media, email, print, and events. Explore the unique strengths and attributes of each channel. Provide guidance on selecting channels that align with business goals and target audience preferences.

Creating a Unified Brand Message

Examine the importance of crafting a unified brand message across channels. Discuss how consistent messaging builds brand recognition and reinforces key brand values. Provide examples of brands effectively maintaining consistency in diverse marketing channels.

Section 3: Integrated Campaign Planning

Developing Integrated Campaign Strategies

Guide readers through the process of developing integrated marketing campaign strategies. Discuss how to align campaign objectives with overall business goals. Provide insights into creating campaigns that leverage the strengths of each channel.

Coordinating Campaign Timing and Messaging

Explore the coordination of campaign timing and messaging across channels. Discuss the importance of synchronized launches and cohesive messaging to create a seamless brand experience. Provide practical tips for campaign planning and execution.

Section 4: Data Integration and Analytics

Centralizing Data for Insights

Discuss the role of data integration in integrated marketing. Explore how centralizing data from various channels provides a comprehensive view of audience behavior and campaign performance. Provide insights into leveraging integrated data for actionable insights.

Utilizing Cross-Channel Analytics

Examine the use of cross-channel analytics to measure integrated campaign performance. Discuss key performance indicators (KPIs) that span multiple channels, such as customer journey analytics. Provide practical tips for interpreting integrated analytics data.

Section 5: Customer Journey Mapping

Mapping the Customer Journey Across Channels

Explore the concept of customer journey mapping in integrated marketing. Discuss how understanding the customer's path across channels informs targeted engagement strategies. Provide examples of effective customer journey mapping in integrated campaigns.

Personalization and the Customer Journey

Delve into the role of personalization in the integrated customer journey. Discuss how tailoring content and experiences based on customer preferences enhances engagement. Provide insights into using integrated data for personalized marketing.

Section 6: Challenges and Solutions in Integrated Marketing

Overcoming Integration Challenges

Examine common challenges in implementing integrated marketing strategies. Discuss issues such as communication barriers, technology integration, and organizational alignment. Provide practical solutions for overcoming these challenges.

Continuous Improvement in Integration

Explore the concept of continuous improvement in integrated marketing. Discuss the iterative nature of integrated campaigns and the importance of learning from data and audience feedback. Provide strategies for refining integrated strategies over time.

Section 7: Creative Integration Across Channels

Ensuring Creative Consistency

Discuss the importance of creative consistency in integrated marketing. Explore how maintaining a cohesive visual identity, messaging style, and tone across channels reinforces brand recognition. Provide insights into developing a creative framework that adapts to diverse channels.

Tailoring Creatives for Each Channel

Delve into the strategy of tailoring creatives for specific channels. Discuss how different channels have unique requirements and audience expectations. Provide practical tips for adapting visuals and messaging to optimize creative impact in each channel.

Section 8: Social Media Integration

Social Media's Role in Integration

Examine the role of social media in integrated marketing. Discuss how social platforms amplify brand messaging, facilitate engagement, and contribute to a holistic customer experience. Provide examples of successful social media integration in integrated campaigns.

Coordinating Social Media Campaigns

Guide readers through the coordination of social media campaigns within an integrated strategy. Discuss how social media calendars align with overall campaign schedules. Provide insights into leveraging user-generated content across social channels.

Integrating Influencer Marketing

Discuss the integration of influencer marketing into an integrated strategy. Explore how influencers can amplify brand messages and reach new audiences across various channels. Provide insights into selecting influencers aligned with campaign objectives.

Measuring Influencer Impact

Examine methods for measuring the impact of influencer marketing within an integrated campaign. Discuss metrics such as reach, engagement, and conversions. Provide practical tips for tracking and evaluating influencer performance.

Section 10: Future Directions in Integrated Marketing

Emerging Trends in Integration

Discuss current and emerging trends in integrated marketing. Explore topics such as the integration of artificial intelligence in personalized campaigns, the rise of immersive technologies, and the evolving role of voice search. Provide insights into staying ahead of integration trends.

The Evolution of Multichannel Experiences

Examine potential future developments in creating multichannel brand experiences. Discuss how advancements in technology may shape the integration of augmented reality (AR), virtual reality (VR), and interactive content. Encourage readers to embrace evolving technologies for a seamless multichannel experience.

Conclusion

Integrated Marketing Excellence: A Journey of Innovation

Summarize the key takeaways from the chapter, emphasizing that integrated marketing excellence is a journey marked by innovation, coordination, and adaptation. Reinforce the idea that the dynamic nature of the marketing landscape requires ongoing integration and a commitment to staying ahead of trends. Conclude by highlighting the enduring value of integrated marketing as a transformative force in achieving marketing goals.

www.ingramcontent.com/pod-product-compliance
Lightning Source LLC
Chambersburg PA
CBHW062239290526
45794CB00006B/2349